JIM EDWARDS

Motivational Guide

The Ultimate Motivation Guide to Success

First edition

This book was professionally typeset on Reedsy.
Find out more at reedsy.com

Contents

#1 SECRET OF SUCCESS   1

WANT TO BE SUCCESSFUL, STOP MAKING EXCUSES!   3

STEPS TO OBTAINING SUCCESS FOR YOUR PERSONAL & BUSINESS LIFE   5

SOMETIMES IT'S THE SMALL THINGS THAT COUNT   11

WHAT ARE YOUR HABITS SAYING ABOUT YOU?   14

LEARNING TO BREAK OR MAKE HABITS   16

NO ONE CAN DO EVERYTHING FIRST   19

5 TIPS TO MOTIVATION MAGNIFICATION   22

10 STEPS TO SELF-MOTIVATION & SALES   25

TAKING CARE OF YOURSELF   30

SELF ESTEEM   33

THE IMPORTANCE OF ENCOURAGEMENT   36

CONCLUSION: THE A-Z OF MOTIVATION   38

MOTIVATIONAL QUOTES   43

#1 SECRET OF SUCCESS

QUOTE: *"Failure Will Never Overtake Me If My Determination To Succeed Is Strong Enough."-Og Mandino-*

Do you know what one of the key secrets of success is – what makes people successful in business, sport or any other aspect of their lives? Let me come back to that in a minute. Ever since I discovered that I wasn't invincible and that my body would fall apart over time, I've been a member of a gym. I've attended regularly over the past fifteen years and my body deterioration is almost being kept in check.

However I've always noticed a lot of new faces at the gym, some of which seem to disappear over a short period of time. Most gyms and health clubs have a high turnover of members or "churn" as the marketing people like to call it. One club I know of loses around fifty members a month and has to work hard to sign up that number just for the business to stand still.

It's not that these gyms offer a poor service, on the contrary – it's because the members – "give up."

New members join to lose weight or to get fit. They then torture themselves on the rowing machines and all the other instruments of agony. If, after a few weeks of sweat and pain, they don't see any visible result – they give up.

You're probably away ahead of me on this; because the key secret of success

1

that I mentioned earlier is this – NEVER EVER GIVE UP. This is what separates the winners from the losers in business, in sport and in life – this is what success is all about. If you have a mountain to climb either literally or figuratively and you reach an obstacle – don't give up. Find another way round – even go back a short distance and come at the situation from another direction.

Whatever it is you're trying to achieve, whatever success you want – never give up! Make mistakes – fall down – get up – fall down – but get up and try again. So there you have it – If you want success remember what Winston Churchill once said – "Never – Never – Never give up!"

Quote: "I've missed more than 9000 shots in my career. I've lost almost 300 games. 26 times I've been trusted to take the game winning shot and missed. I've failed over and over and over again in my life. And that is why I succeed."
-Michael Jordan-

Now that you have the main key to success, keep reading for more tips, encouragement and motivational quotes that will take you to the top. Whether you're looking for success in your business or personal life this book will help you achieve overall success.

WANT TO BE SUCCESSFUL, STOP MAKING EXCUSES!

QUOTE: *"I attribute my success to this: I never gave or took any excuse."-Florence Nightingale-*

Excuses! Excuses! When we fail to do something we are expected to do, we almost always have an excuse for it. However, if we analyze it closely, an excuse is a self-destructive alibi for having failed to do something, especially when it involves attaining a goal. Instead of trying to persevere in finding ways to continue achieving a goal, some of us resort to excuses. Even a handicap cannot be used as an excuse. Many handicapped but determined people have become achievers and champions. Instead of using a handicap as an excuse, let us turn it into an asset. Let us explore this further.

A handicap need not be a reason for failure. On the contrary, a handicap can be a reason for success. People with a handicap always have an offsetting strength that allows them to overcome problems better than others. A person with a handicap has one obsession – to lead a normal life. Depending on the handicap, a person would prefer to be as independent as possible. So he struggles and finds ways to overcome his impediment. When he is able to achieve his goal, this raises his self-esteem. In turn, he inspires others. Everybody has handicaps in varying forms and degree. That is why; it requires effort and determination to overcome them. Handicaps can either be physical, financial, or emotional. And they can either be real or imagined.

Whenever we look at a handicap, we almost always look on the negative side only. Its about time we take a look at the positive side of it. The positive side may be the difficult side, but its the one worth looking into. Its the side that is going to lead us to excel in life. If you think your handicap is physical, like having a weak body, you can counteract this through proper diet and training exercises. As long as the physical parts of your body are intact and mobile, there's no reason why you cannot make it strong and useful. Why? Even those without a leg (for example) can be made to walk or run normally. With the advancement of science, artificial legs can help a handicap function with great mobility.

It your handicap is financial, then the more reason you have to rise above your present status. And if your financial status limits your educational attainment to improve your life, the school is not the only place to learn. Certainly, there are help centers to get you started even from zero level. Once you are initially warmed up with the basics of an education, the rest is up to you. Make use of libraries. Once you are educationally equipped, use your brain and come up with creative ideas to improve your life. If you are emotionally disturbed with negative thoughts, it is like you are sitting on a chair with wobbling legs. Try sitting on a chair with sturdy legs; meaning, look at the bright, positive side of life. Put aside negativity and start thinking positively. The only one who can stop you is yourself.

If your handicap is a combination of any of the physical, financial, or emotional type, congratulations. You should strive more to overcome them, because a double layer of perseverance results to more than double the achievement. Where the odds are greater, the prize gets much bigger. After all the efforts you have exerted, the prize of success shall be a well-deserved one. So whats your excuse for not being successful?

QUOTE: *"Successful people do what unsuccessful people are not willing to do. Don't wish it were easier; wish you were better."-Jim Rohn-*

STEPS TO OBTAINING SUCCESS FOR YOUR PERSONAL & BUSINESS LIFE

QUOTE: "Success usually comes to those who are too busy to be looking for it."-Henry David Thoreau-

Fact: Success is something of which we all want more.

Fact: Most people believe that success is difficult.

Fact: They're wrong – its not!

Success isn't really that difficult. There is a significant portion of the population here in North America, that actually want and need success to be hard! Why? So they then have a built-in excuse when things don't go their way! Pretty sad situation, to say the least. For those of you who are serious about having more, doing more, giving more and being more, success is achievable with some understanding of what to do, some discipline around planning and execution of those plans and belief that you can achieve your desires.

The Truth About Success

The first thing to remember about success is that it is a process nothing more, nothing less. There is really no magic to it and its not reserved only for a select few people. As such, success really has nothing to do with luck, coincidence or fate. It really comes down to understanding the steps in the process and then executing on those steps. There are basically six key areas to higher achievement. Some people will tell you there are four while others may tell you there are eight. One thing for certain though, is that irrespective of the number of steps the experts talk about, they all originate from the same roots. From my perspective then, here are the six key steps:

1. Making the decision
   2. Clarity – developing the Vision
   3. Focus having a plan
   4. Commitment understanding the price and having the willingness to pay that price
   5. Belief believing in yourself and those around you
   6. Taking action practice Ready, Fire, Aim

Making the Decision

If success is a process with a number of defined steps, then it is just like any other process. So, what is the first step in any process? Making a decision to do something this is the first step. We all know that nothing moves until someone makes a decision. The first action is always in making the decision to proceed. This is a fundamental step, which most people overlook. So, make the decision to move forward. Commit your decision to paper, just to bring it into focus. Then, go for it!

Clarity

Having clarity of purpose and a clear picture of what you desire, is probably the single most important factor in achievement. Why is Clarity so important? Without clarity, you send a very garbled message out to the Universe. We know that the Law of Attraction says that we will attract what we focus on, so if we don't have clarity, we will attract confusion.

Consider the following analogy:

You are going on a cruise, but when the ship sets sail, you discover it has no rudder. What happens? One of 3 things will occur:

1. You will sail along until you collide with an immovable object, after which you will sink to the bottom
　　2. You will run aground and become hopelessly stuck in the mud
　　3. You will drift aimlessly until you arrive back at the original dock

Trying to go through life without clarity is similar to sailing a rudder-less ship no good thing can or will happen! The sad thing is the majority of people have no clue about what they truly want. They have no clarity. When asked the question, responses will be superficial at best, and at worst, will be what someone else wants for them.

So how do we get clarity? Simply by asking ourselves lots of questions: What do I really want? What does success look like to me? Why do I want a particular thing? How will this achievement change my life? How can I use this success to make a difference for others?

Introspection is the trick. Understand what you want, why you want it and what it will do for you. This is a critical factor, and as such, is probably the most difficult step. For this reason, most people never complete this aspect then wonder why life is so difficult! Once you have a clear understanding of what you want, it is critical that you engage in goal setting specifically setting SMART goals. SMART is an acronym for Specific, Measurable, Achievable, Realistic and Time Sensitive – S-M-A-R-T. Knowing what you want and setting SMART goals as mileposts on your quest cannot help but give you clarity!

Focus

Focus is having the unwavering attention to complete what you set out to do. There are a million distractions in every facet of our lives. Telephones and e-mail, clients and managers, spouses and kids, TV, newspapers and radio the distractions are everywhere and endless. Everyone wants a piece of us and the result can be totally overwhelming. So, how can we stay on course with all the distractions in our lives? Willpower is a good start, but its very difficult to stay on track simply through willpower.

The best way is to develop and follow a plan. Start with your goals in mind and then work backwards to develop the plan. What steps are required to get you to the goals? Make the plan as detailed as possible. Try to visualize and then plan for, every possible setback. Commit the plan to paper and then keep it with you at all times. Review it regularly and ensure that every step takes you closer to your Vision and Goals. If the plan doesnt support the vision then change it!

Along with your plans, you should consider developing an action orientation that will keep you motivated to move forward at all times. This requires a little self-discipline, but is a crucial component to achievement of any kind. Before starting any new activity, ask yourself if that activity will move you closer to your goals. If the answer is no, you may want to reconsider doing it at that time.

I coach my clients to practice the 3 Ds Defer, Delegate or Delete. Can the particular activity be done later? Defer it! Can it be done by someone else? Delegate it! Does it need to be done at all? If not, consider deleting it! Posing these questions will help to keep you focused on what is truly important!

Commitment

Commitment is something that comes from understanding that everything has its price and then having the willingness to pay that price. This is important because nobody wants to put significant effort into something, only to find out after the fact that the price was too high. The price is something not necessarily defined as financial. It could be time, effort, sacrifice, money or perhaps, something else. The point is that we must be fully aware of the price and be willing to pay it, if we want to have success.

Belief

This is perhaps the single biggest obstacle that all of us must overcome in order to be successful. We all carry a lot of baggage, thanks to our upbringing. The majority of people carry with them, an entire series of self-limiting beliefs that will absolutely stop, and hold them back from, success. Things like Im not good enough, Im not smart enough, Im not lucky enough, and the worst, Im not worthy are but a few of the self-limiting beliefs I have encountered. We carry them with us like rocks in a knapsack, and then use them to sabotage our success. So, how twisted is that?!?!

The old expression is absolutely true whether you think you can or you cant, your'e right! One of the main areas that I work on with my clients is shedding these non-supportive beliefs and replacing them with beliefs that will help them to accomplish their desires. It is truly amazing the damage that we, as parents, can inflict on our children. So why do we do it? For the most part, we don't do it intentionally or with malice. In the majority of cases, the cause is a well-meaning but unskilled or un-thinking parent, who says the wrong thing at the wrong time, and the message sticks as simple as that! And it's not just parents that are the cause – teachers, friends, clergy members or anyone else that has influence in a child's life can be a contributor to these self-limiting beliefs! The bottom line is that we must shed the bad and replace with good beliefs.

Taking Action

Nothing changes until something moves this is the battle cry of author and journalist Robert Ringer. And he is absolutely correct. Not all of the decision-making, clarity, planning, focus and belief in the world, will get you to where you want to be, without taking action! Action putting your plans into play that is what will get you to the destination. Dont get caught in the paralysis of analysis, or in the conundrum of Ready, Aim, Aim, Aim, Aim .Get the oars in the water and start rowing. Execution is the single biggest factor in achievement, so the faster and better your execution, the quicker you will get to the goals!

QUOTE: *"Take up one idea. Make that one idea your life-think of it, dream of it, live on that idea. Let the brain, muscles, nerves, every part of your body, be full of that idea, and just leave every other idea alone. This is the way to success." -Swami Vivekananda-*

SOMETIMES IT'S THE SMALL THINGS THAT COUNT

QUOTE: The small change that creates massive results in your life. "It is never too late to become what you might have been." – GEORGE ELIOT-

I believe that we all reach certain key points in our lives. We all reach crossroads where our lives hit a certain threshold of "pain" that we are no longer willing to settle for. This threshold is very different for every person. I also believe that if you are unhappy with anything in your life then that is a call to action; a desire from deep within the "real" you that wants to experience more of life. This can be very challenging for a lot of people as they have this urge to improve their lives but they don't have an effective strategy. They then do the "logical" thing which is to work on the effects instead of the cause. Here is a simple thought process that will be a wake up call to you if you feel like you are spinning your wheels.

For my life to get better I have to get better. For things to change I have to change.
I am mine. This is my life and I am the creator of my destiny. I can change any and everything in my life by simply changing myself. This puts me in the driving seat of my life and makes my life my responsibility. It eliminates fear and apprehension for I know that no matter what life gives me I can always get to the next level and take the next step by simply making the internal shift in my own psychology.

I can stop looking for events, people and circumstances to blame. I only need to look inside. No matter how influential you are you cannot control the circumstances and events of your life. There are only three things over which you have absolute and total control and these are all you need. It forms the total experience of life. My thoughts, my actions and my words are always under my conscious control. They are MY thoughts, they are MY actions and they are MY words AND they create MY world every minute of every day.

This is incredibly liberating. Whenever I want to have more, experience more or change anything, I need only look inwards and work on myself. Jim Rohn once said that the hardest work you will ever do is the work you do on yourself. See, you can run around and work incredibly hard at trying to influence and change circumstances, but that will only make you tired and discourage your future efforts. Its much easier to change yourself and your perception of yourself and your life. Nothing has any meaning except for the meaning you give it.

Changing external events have very little impact in your life on the long term. Small changes in you; in your perceptions and psychology might seem insignificant at first, but because the change is in you it effects all of your thoughts, all of your actions and all of your words. This seemingly insignificant change, over time changes the whole direction and end destination of your life. If a captain of a ship changes direction just one degree the end destination might be a different continent all together. Like the captain changing his course by one degree it might be unnoticeable over a short period of time, but over greater distances the small change becomes very significant.

Most people try and change the big things; they constantly try and change any and everything in their lives, but they then fail to maintain the change. Instead, making small consistent changes in yourself, in your own character you can create phenomenal results. All change starts and ends with you. If you are going to invest the time and effort to improve your life, then invest it in changing yourself. Invest your time and effort in improving "you" and let go of the superficial urges to control events and circumstances. Your whole perception and experience of life comes from you and who you are. Change yourself, improve your character and just watch the world improve and change before your very eyes.

QUOTE: To change your world, begin with your thoughts - Norman Vincent Peale

WHAT ARE YOUR HABITS SAYING ABOUT YOU?

We are what our habits make us. They are either moving us forward or holding us back. Unfortunately, when it comes to habits, its much easier to form bad habits than it is a good habit. This is because bad habits are usually easy to do. They take little effort. On the other hand, a good habit requires effort and self-discipline. They are much more difficult to acquire.

QUOTE: *All our life, so far as it has definite form, is but a mass of habits – practical, emotional, and intellectual – systematically organized, for our weal or woe, and bearing us irresistibly toward our destiny whatever it may be.-Theron Dumont-*

Negative habits are time wasting, character eroding, and health destroying. Once developed. A bad habit is difficult to overcome. Once overcome, one must be constantly on guard against slipping back into it. Unlike bad habits, a good habit is much easier to let go. Maintaining a good habit demands constant attention. It would be much easier to not have formed the bad habit in the first place, but unfortunately, they are often formed in youth, when one lacks the foresight to see ahead the consequences of their actions. Good habits, once developed, are what drive a person toward success and accomplishment.

QUOTE: *We are what we repeatedly do. Excellence then, is not an act but a habit. – Aristotle-*

One thing that can help keep you adhering to your good habits is to keep your eye on the big picture. Keep in mind that each daily task accomplished is moving you toward your goals. It takes about thirty days to form a habit. Once a good habit has been developed, a person feels uncomfortable and ill at ease if he neglects it. Instead of a burden, a new good habit becomes a comfort and a joy. Don't be discouraged if you slip up, either by neglecting a good habit or falling back into a bad one. Just pick yourself up and get back on the right track. Admonish yourself to show more resolve but don't torture yourself and fall into a hopeless depression.

QUOTE: *The greatest glory is in never falling, but rising when you fall.-Vince Lombardi-*

Don't let people ridicule you for persisting in your good habits. They are just trying to pull you down to their level. You will soon leave them in the dust. People who exercise regularly or try to eat healthy are often derided as being fanatics. Those that criticize are just feeling guilty because they lack the resolve to do what you are doing. Sit down and think for a moment about what habits you may have. What are your good habits? What habits are hindering you? People of character are the ones who have built good habits into their lives and have eliminated the bad ones. It is your life and your responsibility to govern yourself. You are the master of your ship.

LEARNING TO BREAK OR MAKE HABITS

QUOTE: "Success is the sum of small efforts, repeated day in and day out."
-Robert Collier-

We all have habits, some good and some not so good. These are behaviors that we've learned and that occur almost automatically. And most of us have a habit we'd like to break, or one we'd like to develop. For most people, it takes about four weeks for a new behavior to become routine, or habit. Your daily habits can easily determine your road to success, most successful people have daily rituals. The following steps can make it easier to establish new behavior patterns to get you to the top.

1. The first step is to set your goal. Especially when you are trying to stop or break a habit, you should try to phrase your goal as a positive statement. For example, instead of saying "I will quit snacking at night", say "I will practice healthy eating habits". You should also write down your goal. Committing it to paper helps you to commit. It can also help if you tell your goal to someone you trust.

2. Decide on a replacement behavior. (If your goal is to develop a new habit then your replacement behavior will be the goal itself.) This step is very important when you are trying to break a habit. If you want to stop a

behavior, you must have a superior behavior to put in it's place. If you don't, the old behavior pattern will return.

3. Learn and be aware of your triggers. Behavior patterns don't exist independently. Often, one habit is associated with another part of your regular routine. For instance, in the snacking example the trigger may be late night television or reading. You automatically grab a bag of chips while you watch. Many people who smoke automatically light up after eating. Think about when and why you do the thing you want to quit.

4. Post reminders to yourself. You can do this by leaving yourself notes in the places where the behavior usually occurs. Or you can leave yourself a message on the mirror, refrigerator, computer monitor or some other place where you will see it regularly. You can also have a family member or co-worker use a particular phrase to remind you of your goal.

5. Get help and support from someone. This is kind of obvious. Any job is easier with help. It works even better if you can form a partnership with someone who shares the same goal.

6. Write daily affirmations. Write your phrase or sentence in the present tense (as if it were already happening), and write it ten times a day for twenty-one days. This process helps make your goal a part of your subconscious, which will not only remind you to practice the new behavior, but it also keeps you focused and motivated.

7. Reward yourself for making progress at set time intervals. Focus on your goal one day at a time, but give yourself a small treat at one, three and six months. The rewards don't have to be big or expensive, and you should try to make it something that's associated in some way with the goal. Doing this provides you with both incentive and extra motivation.
Following these steps is no guarantee of success of course. Depending on the habit it may take several tries to finally make the change. But if you stick

with it, you can do it.

Quote: "Whenever you see a successful person, you only see the public glories, never the private sacrifices to reach them."-Vaibhav Shah-

NO ONE CAN DO EVERYTHING FIRST

Quote: People don't act because a lot of things are in front of them. -Paul Hartunian-

After attending several seminars with so much information you tend to be on information overload. The vast majority of people freeze; then wound up doing nothing at all. All this information from so many experts, willing to help you accomplish what you want to accomplish. They may have offered lots advice and ideas; SO MANY options in one day may cause information overload and cause you to freeze.

The point is that when we're confronted by too many possibilities, we can freeze up. Trying to decide which of 15 or 20 options to pursue can be frustrating, especially if all of them appear to be good choices. My granddaddy used to say, "A dog that chases two rabbits won't catch either one." He'd pause for a second, then add, "And he'll go hungry tonight." He was trying to get me to realize how important it is to just pick one thing and do it. Let's take an example that we often see here on the Internet. How many eBooks have you bought within the last six months? Of that number, how many of them tell you how to do marketing or to make money online?

If a book is any good, you'll be impressed; you'll say, "Yeah, I can do this." But then, after a few days, you'll read another really great sales letter, you'll feel that you really, really need the knowledge in this new offering. Then you'll buy yet another eBook, and you'll again be impressed: "Yeah, I can REALLY do THIS."

This cycle is being repeated over and over every day all around the Internet. This may have happened to you. I've done it. Lots of people have. So there you sit with perhaps dozens of books, all good, dozens or even hundreds of affiliate offerings, some excellent, and page after page of website ideas, all interesting. In fact, you've got so many options that you may not know what to do first.

My granddaddy ran one of the biggest plumbing shops in his town, and when he'd notice one of his men dithering over what to do next, he'd simply say, "Son, you can't do everything first."And neither can you or I. If all your options are good, then it doesn't really matter which one you choose first. Throw a dart if you have to, but move. Make a decision. Get yourself into motion.

For many people, getting into motion means you'll be stepping into unfamiliar territory, doing things you've never done before. So what? At least it's interesting and exciting. But never terrifying. If you think starting your very first business is terrifying, you need to think again. Wrestling a grizzly bear is terrifying. Falling from an airplane without a parachute is terrifying. But starting a business? Nah… that's not scary; it's just unfamiliar. And right there we have the main reason most people lock up when they face a long list of options. It's unfamiliar ground, so they think they don't know how to choose. (They do, but they THINK they don't.)

Here's a strategy for taking the terror out of decision-making. Take that long list of options. Say there are 15 items on it, and you've never done any of them before. Once you've examined all the items on the list, do this: Decide if all the items are REALLY about equal. If there are any that clearly don't measure up, cross those off. You'll still be left with lots of choices. Let's say you're left with only 10 items on your list. Take out a new sheet of paper.

Write item number one on it, the first item from your original list.

Okay, that's it. That's your new list of options – just one item. We've already agreed that all the choices are more or less equal. So now you've got your action agenda. One item. No more indecision. Now just go do it. And those other 9 items? They'll be there waiting when you get done with the first task. See how easy decision-making can be?

QUOTE: "You miss 100% of the shots you don't take".-Wayne Gretzky-

5 TIPS TO MOTIVATION MAGNIFICATION

"Nothing is impossible, the word itself says, "I'm possible!" -*Audrey Hepburn*-

Motivation is the driving force behind life-enhancing change. It comes from knowing exactly what you want to do and having an insatiable, burning desire to do whats necessary to get it. It keeps your dream on track as it is the power of motivation that keeps you going when the going gets tough.

Here's 5 top tips to help you magnify your motivation:

1. Create a picture board and fill it with images of your desired goals. The car you want to own, the house you want to live in, the area where you want to live yes, they're the obvious ones. Others could be pictures of holiday destinations, trophies, first-class travel tickets, clothes you want to buy, fine restaurants you want to frequent whatever you can think of that gets your pulse racing.

2. GET ANGRY. If you want to change your life for the better then get angry about where you're at now. Having a bias attitude towards change isn't whats needed and it wont create a strong desire within you. So ask: Why do I want to change? Is it because you're FED UP with debts? Does your job DRIVE YOU CRAZY? Is your life DULL AND PREDICTABLE? Are you SICK AND

TIRED of doing the same thing week in week out? Are you BORED BEYOND BELIEF by the dull, uninspiring, unhappy people you associate with? THEN GET ANGRY ABOUT IT. And I mean REAL ANGRY. Write it all down, all of the frustrating, unrewarding, miserable things that make you unhappy.

3. Appreciate the value of time! Time is one of the most precious resources you have and it is also a NON RENEWABLE resource. You can either use it fully or squander it. If you want to create change you're going to have to invest a lot of time to make it happen. Start to reduce the time you waste on irrelevancies: Television, newspapers, lie-ins, weekends spent shopping, partying, dining out, visiting an endless line of relatives and friends these wont help you get what you want and all of them will rob time from you. Valuable time that you can use much more effectively by investing it in YOU. Remember this: You have a finite amount of time here on Earth. You don't know how much time you have no one does. But its how you use the time you have that counts. So make your time count and that means starting from right NOW.

4. Conformity. Are you a mindless person who's way too timid to pursue your own way? Do you have to follow where everyone else goes, doing exactly what everyone else does and therefore, who gets the same levels of happiness as all the other people? Seriously, does this describe YOU? Are you too frightened to be different than everyone else because they wouldn't like it if you decided to follow a different path? So you dutifully go along following everyone else because if they're doing it then it must be right? But if you do what everyone else does you'll just get what everyone else gets. No one wants to be considered mindless, or a timid individual who blindly follows others? You probably prefer to be a leader, a warrior who possesses the courage to be uniquely you and to do what you want to do and make your dreams happen? If so, this means you have to be more like a tiger than a sheep. Do you really want to be a sheep? I mean, haven't we got enough sheep already?

5. Fear your fear. Fear is the force that is determined to stop you in your

tracks and rob your dreams from you. But it can only do this if you let it. Don't let this cruel destructive charlatan wreck your dreams, steal your happiness or crush your spirit? Imagine this thought haunting your final days: I didn't do the things I wanted because I was too frightened to live. And by then, it'll be far too late to conquer fear. Refuse to let fear spoil your life and start taking action now!

The world is waiting for your unique gifts. Why keep it waiting any longer?

QUOTE: *"You may be disappointed if you fail, but you are doomed if you don't try."*
  -Beverly Sills-

10 STEPS TO SELF-MOTIVATION & SALES

QUOTE: The question should not be who is going to let you, but who is going to try and stop you -Ayn Rand-

Every day of your life you are selling yourself, nothing happens until you're successful at doing that. We're all in the selling business whether we like it or not. It doesn't matter whether you're a lawyer or an accountant, a manager or a politician, an engineer or a doctor. We all spend a great deal of our time trying to persuade people to buy our product or service, accept our proposals or merely accept what we say. Before you get better at persuading or influencing other people – you need to get better at self-motivation and selling yourself.

Here are 10 simple steps to self-motivation:

#1 – You must believe in the product

Selling yourself is pretty much like selling anything. Firstly, you need to believe in what you're selling. That means believing in "you." It's about lots of positive self-talk and the right attitude. The first thing people notice about you is your attitude. If you're like most people then you'll suffer from lack of confidence from time to time. It really all comes down to how you talk to yourself. The majority of people are more likely to talk to themselves negatively than positively – this is what holds them back in life.It isn't just about a positive attitude; it's about the right attitude – the quality of your thinking.

Successful people have a constructive and optimistic way of looking at themselves and their work. They have an attitude of calm, confident, positive self-expectation. They feel good about themselves and believe that everything they do will lead to their inevitable success.If you're in a sales job or a business owner or a manager then you need to continually work on your attitude. You need to listen to that little voice inside your head. Is it saying you're on top, going for it and confident, or is it holding you back.

If you're hearing – "I can't do this or that" or "They won't want to buy at the moment" or "We're too expensive" then you'd better change your self-talk or change your job. Start to believe in yourself and don't let things that are out with your control effect your attitude. Avoid criticizing, condemning and complaining and start spreading a little happiness.

Remember the saying of Henry Ford, founder of the Ford Motor Company – "If you believe you can do a thing, or if you believe you can't, in either case you're probably right."

#2 – The packaging must grab attention

Like any other product we buy, the way the product is packaged and presented will influence the customer's decision to buy. Everything about you needs to look good and you must dress appropriately for the occasion. And don't think that just because your customer dresses casually, that they expect you to dress the same way. The style and colour of the clothes you wear, your spectacles, shoes, briefcase, watch, the pen you use, all make a statement about you.

#3 – Smile

No need to get carried away, you don't need a big cheesy grin, just a pleasant open face that doesn't frighten people away.

#4 – Use names

Use the customers name as soon as you can but don't over do it. Business is less formal nowadays however be careful of using first names initially. Make sure your customer knows yours and remembers it. You can do the old repeat trick -"My name is Bond, James Bond" or "My name is James, James Bond"

#5 – Watch the other person

What does their body language tell you? Are they comfortable with you or are they a bit nervous? Are they listening to you or are their eyes darting around the room. If they're not comfortable and not listening then there's no point telling them something important about your business. Far better to make some small talk and more importantly -get then to talk about themselves. It's best to go on the assumption that in the first few minutes of meeting someone new, they won't take in much of what you say. They're too busy analyzing all the visual data they're taking in.

#6 – Listen and look like you're listening.

Many people, particularly men, listen but don't show that they're listening. The other person can only go on what they see, not what's going on inside your head. If they see a blank expression then they'll assume you're "out to lunch." The trick is to do all the active listening things such as nodding your head, the occasional "UH-HUH" and the occasional question.

#7 – Be interested.

If you want to be INTERESTING then be INTERESTED. This really is the most important thing you can do to be successful at selling yourself. The majority of people are very concerned about their self-image. If they sense that you value them, that you feel that they're important and worth listening to, then you effectively raise their self-image. If you can help people to like themselves then they'll LOVE you. Don't fall into the trap of flattering the other person, because most people will see right through you and they won't fall for it. Just show some genuine interest in the customer and their business and they'll be much more receptive to what you say.

#8 – Talk positively.

Don't say – "Isn't it a horrible day" or "Business is pretty tough at present" or any thing else that pulls the conversation down. Say things like (and only the truth) – "I like the design of this office" or "I've heard some good reports about your new product."

#9 – Mirror the other person

This doesn't mean mimicking the other person, it just means you speaking and behaving in a manner that is similar to the customer. For example, if your customer speaks slowly or quietly, then you speak slowly or quietly. Remember people like people who are like themselves.

#10 – Warm and friendly

If you look or sound stressed or aggressive then don't be surprised if the other person gets defensive and less than willing to co-operate. If you look and sound warm and friendly, then you're more likely to get a positive response. This isn't about being all nicey-nicey. It's about a pleasant open face or a warm tone over the telephone. Before we can get down to the process of selling our product, our service or our ideas then we need to be as sure as we can be – that the customer has bought us and that we have their full attention.

QUOTE: *"The difference between ordinary and extraordinary is that little extra."-Jimmy Johnson-*

TAKING CARE OF YOURSELF

Living in our world today can be very stressful. While some of the stress that we experience is actually useful for motivating us, a point can be reached where it becomes very harmful, physically, emotionally and even spiritually. Knowing how to manage and even reduce the harmful effects of stress on a daily basis, of staying balanced and centered as we encounter the many stressors of everyday living, is crucial to our well being. Among other things, taking care of ourselves will necessarily involve us nurturing our physical body, of eating healthy foods, of exercising. Learning how to take care of ourselves in this respect is also very important for everyone as our experience of stress can and does affect others as well.

Learning how to take care of ourselves also involves making appropriate distinctions about ourselves, others and life in general. One distinction that is crucial for our well being is realizing how and from where much of our stress is primarily generated. While some of the stressors that we face are apart of what it is to be a human being, much of the stress that we experience is of our own creation.

A great deal of the stress that we experience has its origin in our own personal story and the meaning we make about life, in the thoughts that we think. Once we understand that we are truly the cause in the matter, that we are responsible for the thoughts that we create or invent and that it is from these thoughts that much of our stress is generated, then and only then will we begin to be able to truly manage our stress and have the power to live the life that we want and love. Blaming others or situations for that which we experience will only limit our power, lead to frustration and eventually a great deal of stress.

Becoming present to the fact that we have a tendency to constantly evaluate, judge and even blame others, and especially ourselves, is very important. How we conceive of others and ourselves in this respect will make a huge difference in our experience of life. For example, for some much of their life is spent attempting to make others and themselves wrong, wrong for what they think and do, wrong for what we think and do.

Once we make another wrong, especially ourselves, anger, anxiety, guilt, frustration and even sadness will eventually follow and with it a great deal of stress. A simple truth is that as human beings we are all doing the best that we can at any given moment. If we or others knew differently we would behave differently.

Another simple truth is that we are perfect, whole and complete just as we are. It is our story about ourselves that does not allow us to truly experience our own completeness. Making mistakes in life does not make us wrong or flawed in some way but only presents us with feedback and valuable opportunities for growth. Becoming present to how we make ourselves wrong, of how we put ourselves down, allows us an opening to realize that we are not what we do or think.

Our true self is something much different. Becoming present to our attempts to make others and ourselves wrong in some manner will also create a cleaning for us to begin to think, feel and behave differently. Once we fully realize that we are perfect, whole and complete just as are, we will bring forth into our lives experiences that will truly empower us and others. It will be at this point that we will begin to authentically take care of ourselves.

Taking care of ourselves in this respect will also involve taking care of our true self, of unconditionally loving ourselves completely. It is only when we truly love and accept ourselves, as we are, in the present moment that we will be able to do so with others. We always think, feel and behave towards others as we think, feel and act towards ourselves.

One manner in which we can practice being who we truly are is beginning to become aware of the thoughts and beliefs that exist within us including and especially those that are self-limiting. Meditation and other holistic, self-enhancement techniques of this nature allow us this ability and opportunity to watch, monitor and become present to our inner world, to the very thoughts that generate our life and experiences.

Such a process will eventually allow us to truly understand that we are not our thoughts and beliefs, that we are something different from, that we are much more. Our thoughts are merely apart of the machinery of being human.

Once present to the thoughts and beliefs that quickly, if not instantly, move through our mind also allows us the opportunity to reframe from impulsively acting upon them and as a result to become free from their constraints and potential harm to us and others. Such a meditative process, especially as it applies to the thoughts and beliefs that we have about ourselves, is the key to truly taking care of yourself. Such awareness will eventually allow us to truly experience the fact that we are good enough, just as we are, one that deserves to have a wonderful and powerful life, that we truly are perfect, whole and complete.

Once we fully understand this for ourselves it will allow us to get it about others, for those that we work with and for those in our lives that we love. The end result of such a meditative process is that much of the stress that we experience, especially that which we create, will simply not exist, allowing us to create or invent the life that we truly want and love and to live it powerfully.

SELF ESTEEM

Self Esteem plays a huge part in life and can stand in the way of you achieving success if you let it. Here are some tips to stay calm, composed and maintain self esteem in a tough environments? Imagine yourself as a Dart Board. Everything and everyone else around you may become Dart Pins, at one point or another. These dart pins will destroy your self esteem and pull you down in ways you wont even remember. Don't let them destroy you, or get the best of you. So which dart pins should you avoid?

Dart Pin #1 : Negative Work Environment

Beware of dog eat dog theory where everyone else is fighting just to get ahead. This is where non-appreciative people usually thrive. No one will appreciate your contributions even if you miss lunch and dinner, and stay up late. Most of the time you get to work too much without getting help from people concerned. Stay out of this, it will ruin your self esteem. Competition is at stake anywhere. Be healthy enough to compete, but in a healthy competition that is.

Dart Pin #2: Other Peoples Behavior

Bulldozers, brown nosers, gossipmongers, whiners, backstabbers, snipers, people walking wounded, controllers, naggers, complainers, exploders, patronizers, sluffers all these kinds of people will pose bad vibes for your self esteem, as well as to your self improvement scheme.

Dart Pin #3: Changing Environment

You cant be a green bug on a brown field. Changes challenge our paradigms. It tests our flexibility, adaptability and alters the way we think. Changes will make life difficult for awhile, it may cause stress but it will help us find ways to improve our selves. Change will be there forever, we must be susceptible to it. Truthfully, the only difference between you and Self esteem experts is time. If you'll invest a little more time in reading, you'll be that much nearer to expert status when it comes to Self esteem.

Dart Pin #4: Past Experience

Its okay to cry and say ouch! when we experience pain. But don't let pain transform itself into fear. It might grab you by the tail and swing you around. Treat each failure and mistake as a lesson.

Dart Pin #5: Negative World View

Look at what youre looking at. Dont wrap yourself up with all the negativities of the world. In building self esteem, we must learn how to make the best out of worst situations.

Dart Pin #6: Determination Theory

The way you are and your behavioral traits is said to be a mixed end product of your inherited traits (genetics), your upbringing (psychic), and your environmental surroundings such as your spouse, the company, the economy or your circle of friends. You have your own identity. If your father is a failure, it doesnt mean you have to be a failure too. Learn from other peoples experience, so youll never have to encounter the same mistakes. Sometimes, you may want to wonder if some people are born leaders or positive thinkers. NO. Being positive, and staying positive is a choice. Building self esteem and drawing lines for self improvement is a choice, not a rule or a talent. God wouldnt come down from heaven and tell you George, you may now have the permission to build self esteem and improve your self.

In life, its hard to stay tough specially when things and people around you keep pulling you down. When we get to the battle field, we should choose the right luggage to bring and armors to use, and pick those that are bullet proof. Lifes options give us arrays of more options. Along the battle, we will get hit and bruised. And wearing a bullet proof armor ideally means self change. The kind of change which comes from within. Voluntarily. Armor or Self Change changes 3 things: our attitude, our behavior and our way of thinking.

Building self esteem will eventually lead to self improvement if we start to become responsible for who we are, what we have and what we do. Its like a flame that should gradually spread like a brush fire from inside and out. When we develop self esteem, we take control of our mission, values and discipline. Self esteem brings about self improvement, true assessment, and determination. So how do you start putting up the building blocks of self esteem? Be positive. Be contented and happy. Be appreciative. Never miss an opportunity to compliment. A positive way of living will help you build self esteem, your starter guide to self improvement.

There's a lot to understand about Self esteem. We were able to provide you with some of the facts above, but there is still plenty more to write about in subsequent articles.

THE IMPORTANCE OF ENCOURAGEMENT

QUOTE: *"People Who Are Crazy Enough To Think They Can Change The World, Are The Ones Who Do."-Rob Siltanen-*

Everyone has times when they could use some support or motivation from others. That means everyone is a candidate to receive encouragement from you. Look for someone you know who has been disappointed or is going through a tough moment in life. Showing an interest can be very encouraging. It doesn't matter if there is anything you can do to improve or fix the situation. Your encouragement will help give hope that person knowing there is someone who cares.

Look for someone who has been a positive influence. You might look up to this person. I don't believe there is any better way to be encouraged than to hear from someone that you were a tremendous help in some way. Your encouragement will help inspire that person to be a positive influence on others just as he or she was for you.

Look for someone who is putting in a great effort or doing a great job at something. It does not have to be something you are benefiting from. You just have to notice it and show an interest. Your encouragement will reinforce the actions of that individual and may give him or her strength to do even greater things in the future.

Plan to be an encouragement to at least one person today. Encourage that person in your conversations, write an encouraging note, or help him or her in some way. You will find yourself being encouraged at the same time through your gracious act.

QUOTE: "Remember no one can make you feel inferior without your consent." -Eleanor Roosevelt-

CONCLUSION: THE A-Z OF MOTIVATION

Pain may sometimes be the reason why people change. Getting bad grades make you realize that you need to study. Debts remind you of your inability to look for a source of income. Being humiliated gives you the push to speak up and fight for yourself to save your face from the next embarrassment. It may be a bitter experience, a friends tragic story, a great movie, or an inspiring book that will help you to get up and get just the right amount of motivation you need in order to improve yourself.

With all the people trying to pull you down and waiting for you to fail, how can you stay motivated and positive?

Try this A to Z of tips for Motivation

A – Achieving your dreams. Avoid negative people, things and places because they will only drag you down. Eleanor Roosevelt once said, The future belongs to those who believe in the beauty of their dreams.

B – Believe in your self, and in what you can do. Believe in your possibilities and your dreams. Every advancement of humankind has taken place because someone believed in themselves.

C - Consider all of the angles and aspects of everything you encounter, whether it is people or situations. Motivation comes from strength of purpose. Being able to see both points of view will give you more chance of being successful and keeping those around you motivated too.

D - Don't give up and don't give in. Every successful person from J K Rowling to Walt Disney to Sylvester Stallone to Thomas Edison had multiple failures before being successful. Sometimes their failures or rejections ran into the hundreds before they achieved success.

E - Enjoy. Work as if you don't need money. Dance as if nobody's watching. Love as if you never cried. Learn as if you'll live forever. Motivation takes place when people are happy.

F - Family and Friends. Use your family and friends to help you stay motivated. The big football teams have cheerleaders and fans to encourage them. Your family and friends can be your cheerleaders and fans. Use them to keep you going when you feel your motivation drifting.

G - Give that little bit extra. Self improvement happens everywhere all the time, whether you are at home, at work or at school. The difference in effort between excellent and outstanding is small, yet the difference in rewards is massive. Giving that little bit extra can put you into the outstanding.

H - Hang on to your dreams. There may be times when it looks bleak, but hang on to your dreams. The night is darkest just before the dawn. It is at this moment that you are closest to success and 95% of people will give up. Push through this moment and you'll achieve your dreams.

I - Ignore those who try to destroy you. Don't get involved in their dramas or toxicity just walk away. Surround yourself with people who will encourage and support you. Remove those who want to pull you down and watch you fail from your life. You'll find it much easier to stay motivated.

J - Joy and gratitude. Perhaps two of the fundamentals for motivation and success is to be joyful in what you do and grateful for what you have.

K - Keep pushing forwards no matter how hard life may seem. In the toughest moments you can choose to move forwards or to run away. Its your decision one path brings you closer to the success, the other takes you away from it. Which do you want to follow?

L - Learn to love your self. This isn't as easy as it sounds for most people, but by loving yourself you will be happier and more motivated because you will believe you deserve what you achieve.

M - Make things happen. Motivation and success doesn't come from sitting in front of the television drinking coke and eating pizza. Take action and you'll achieve your dreams.

N - Never lie, cheat or steal. Always play a fair game. At the end of the day, if you live a dishonest life, it will come back to you. Living an honest, fair life allows you to be proud of what you do.

O - Open your eyes. Everyone has a set of blinkers that they wear and see everything through them, i.e. how they would like things to be. Look at life with open eyes and see things how they are, and see them how you want them to be. Then take action to make it happen.

P - Practice makes perfect. The more you practice, the better you become. A top sportsman doesn't reach their status through a single practice or game. They practice harder and longer than anyone else, and as such, are rewarded more than anyone else.

Q - Quitters never win. And winners never quit. So, which do you want to be?

R - Ready yourself. Always be ready to take advantage of the opportunities and situations presented to you. Prepare in advance, and ignore the voice telling you to put it off until tomorrow. Remember, it wasn't raining when Noah built the ark!

S - Stop procrastinating. You can put it all off until tomorrow, but one day there will be no more tomorrows. Start procrastinating about procrastinating and do tomorrows jobs today.

T - Take control of your life. Discipline and self control are synonymous with motivation. So many people believe their lives are out of their control. Look at your life in detail and you'll discover you have more areas under your control than you think.

U - Understand others. If you know very well how to talk, you should also learn how to listen. You have two ears and one mouth for a reason. Understand others and strive to be understood.

V - Visualize it. Your sub-conscious knows no difference between your imagination and reality, so if you rehearse your success in your mind, then your sub-conscious will believe in it and make it happen.

W -Want it more than anything. Every successful person has had a burning desire to achieve their goals. The Wright brothers didn't invent the aeroplane because there was nothing on the television. They had a burning desire to succeed and kept going, even in the face of setbacks.

X - X Factor is what will make you different from the others. When you are motivated, you tend to put on extras on your life like extra time for family, extra help at work, extra care for friends. This X-Factor sets you aside from the crowd and marks you out for success.

Y - You are unique. No one in this world looks, acts, thinks or talks like you.

Value your unique gifts, whatever they are and use them for your success.

Z - Zero in on your dreams and make it happen!!!

Conclusion: So, there you have it; the steps that will help you achieve success! You now have the opportunity to push ahead and reach your potential. No more excuses – make the commitment to take action TODAY! Figure out what you want, put a plan together to achieve it, understand the cost, believe in yourself then go and get it! If you are still struggling with motivation, the last chapter is filled with motivational quotes from some of the greatest of our time.

MOTIVATIONAL QUOTES

Success usually comes to those who are too busy to be looking for
    it."

-Henry David Thoreau-

"Twenty years from now you will be more disappointed by the things that
you didn't do than by the ones you did do, so throw off the bowlines, sail
away from safe harbor, catch the trade winds in your sails. Explore, Dream,
Discover."
-Mark Twain-

"If you are not willing to risk the usual, you will have to settle for the
ordinary."
-Jim Rohn-

"When one door of happiness closes, another opens, but often we look so
long at the closed door that we do not see the one that has been opened for
us."

-Helen Keller-

"I am not a product of my circumstances. I am a product of my decisions."
-Stephen Covey-

"When I stand before God at the end of my life, I would hope that I would not have a single bit of talent left and could say, I used everything you gave me."
-Erma Bombeck-

"Every child is an artist. The problem is how to remain an artist once he grows up."
-Pablo Picasso-

"Life is about making an impact, not making an income"
-Kevin Kruse-

"You can never cross the ocean until you have the courage to lose sight of the shore."

-Christopher Columbus-

"I've learned that people will forget what you said, people will forget what you did, but people will never forget how you made them feel."
-Maya Angelou-

"Life is 10% what happens to me and 90% of how I react to it."
-Charles Swindoll-

"Either you run the day, or the day runs you. "
-Jim Rohn-

"Take up one idea. Make that one idea your life-think of it, dream of it, live on that idea. Let the brain, muscles, nerves, every part of your body, be full of that idea, and just leave every other idea alone. This is the way to success."
-Swami Vivekananda-

"We become what we think about."

-Earl Nightingale-

"Whether you think you can or you think you can't, you're right."
-Henry Ford-

"If you are willing to do more than you are paid to do, eventually you will be paid to do more than you do."
-Anonymous-

"The most common way people give up their power is by thinking they don't have any."
-Alice Walker-

"Success is walking from failure to failure with no loss of enthusiasm."
-Winston Churchill-

"The two most important days in your life are the day you are born and the day you find out why."
-Mark Twain-

"I've missed more than 9000 shots in my career. I've lost almost 300 games. 26 times I've been trusted to take the game winning shot and missed. I've failed over and over and over again in my life. And that is why I succeed."
-Michael Jordan-

"Life isn't about getting and having, it's about giving and being."
-Kevin Kruse-

"Don't Let Yesterday Take Up Too Much Of Today."
-Will Rogers-

"Whatever you can do, or dream you can, begin it. Boldness has genius, power and magic in it."
-Johann Wolfgang von Goethe-

"Whenever you see a successful person, you only see the public glories, never the private sacrifices to reach them."
-Vaibhav Shah-

"The mind is everything. What you think you become."
-Buddha-

"People often say that motivation doesn't last. Well, neither does bathing.
That's why we recommend it daily."
-Zig Zigla-

"The best revenge is massive success."
-Frank Sinatra-

"Try not to become a person of success, but rather try to become a person of
value."
-Albert Einstein-

"If you hear a voice within you say "you cannot paint," then by all means
paint and that voice will be silenced."
-Vincent Van Gogh-

"I attribute my success to this: I never gave or took any excuse."
-Florence Nightingale-

"Ask and it will be given to you; search, and you will find; knock and the door will be opened for you."
-Jesus-

"Failure Will Never Overtake Me If My Determination To Succeed Is Strong Enough."
-Og Mandino-

"The best time to plant a tree was 20 years ago. The second best time is now."
-Chinese Proverb-

"Few things can help an individual more than to place responsibility on him, and to let him know that you trust him."
-Booker T. Washington-

"The most difficult thing is the decision to act, the rest is merely tenacity.
-Amelia Earhart-

"It is not the strongest of the species that survive, nor the most intelligent, but the one most responsive to change."
-Charles Darwin-

"An unexamined life is not worth living."
-Socrates-

"By looking at what you already have in your life, you will always get more. By looking at what you don't have in life, you will never have enough"
- Oprah Winfrey-

"Whatever the mind of man can conceive and believe, it can achieve. "
-Napoleon Hill-

"Great minds discuss ideas; average minds discuss events; small minds discuss people."
-Eleanor Roosevelt-

"Eighty percent of success is showing up."
-Woody Allen-

"You miss 100% of the shots you don't take. "
-Wayne Gretzky-

"No one can make you feel inferior without your consent."
-Eleanor Roosevelt-

"The distance between insanity and genius is measured only by success."
-Bruce Feirstein-

"Go confidently in the direction of your dreams. Live the life you have imagined."
-Henry David Thoreau-

"Your time is limited, so don't waste it living someone else's life."
-Steve Jobs-

"Don't be afraid to give up the good to go for the great."
-John D. Rockefeller-

"Two roads diverged in a wood, and I—I took the one less traveled by, And that has made all the difference. "
–Robert Frost-

"If you can't explain it simply, you don't understand it well enough."
-Albert Einstein-

"There are two types of people who will tell you that you cannot make a difference in this world: those who are afraid to try and those who are afraid you will succeed."
-Ray Goforth-

"Winning isn't everything, but wanting to win is."
-Vince Lombardi-

"Success is the sum of small efforts, repeated day in and day out."
-Robert Collier-

"Courage is resistance to fear, mastery of fear — not absence of fear."
-Mark Twain-

"Only put off until tomorrow what you are willing to die having left undone."
-Pablo Picasso-

"Strive not to be a success, but rather to be of value. "
-Albert Einstein-

"Twenty years from now, you will be more disappointed by the things that you didn't do than by the ones you did do. So throw off the bowlines. Sail away from the safe harbor. Catch the trade winds in your sails. Explore. Dream. Discover."
-Mark Twain-

"Life is what happens to you while you're busy making other plans."
-John Lennon-

Nothing is impossible. In the word, you find that it says, "I'm possible!"
- Audrey Hepburn-

People may forget your words, your actions but they will never forget the feelings that you gave them
-Maya Angelou-

"In life, 10% is what happens to you and 90% is how you react to it"

- Charles Swindoll-

"No one can make you feel small without your permission"
-Eleanor Roosevelt-

"The successful warrior is the average man, with laser like focus."
-Bruce Lee-

"You can't connect the dots looking forward; you can only connect them looking backward. So you have to trust that the dots will somehow connect in your future. You have to trust in something — your gut, destiny, life, karma, whatever. This approach has never let me down, and it has made all the difference in my life."
-Steve Jobs-

"Successful people do what unsuccessful people are not willing to do. Don't wish it were easier; wish you were better."
-Jim Rohn-

"The No. 1 reason people fail in life is because they listen to their friends, family, and neighbors."
-Napoleon Hill-

"You may have to fight a battle more than once to win it."
-Margaret Thatcher-

"Many of life's failures are people who did not realize how close they were to success when they gave up."
-Thomas A. Edison-

"Every strike brings me closer to the next home run."
-Babe Ruth-

"Definiteness of purpose is the starting point of all achievement."
-W. Clement Stone-

"What would you attempt to do if you knew you would not fail?"
-Robert Schuller-

"Always bear in mind that your own resolution to success is more important than any other one thing."
-Abraham Lincoln-

"Successful and unsuccessful people do not vary greatly in their abilities.
They vary in their desires to reach their potential."
John Maxwell

"I've learned that people will forget what you said, people will forget what
you did, but people will never forget how you made them feel."
-Maya Angelou-

"If you think you can or you can't, you are right"
-Henry Ford-

It is not possible to attain perfection but by chasing it, we can attain
excellence
-Vince Lombardi-

"Much of the stress that people feel doesn't come from having too much to
do. It comes from not finishing what they've started."
-David Allen-

"Focus on the journey, not the destination. Joy is found not in finishing an activity but in doing it."
-Greg Anderson-

"You never regret being kind."
-Nicole Shepherd-

"Success at the highest level comes down to one question: Can you decide that your happiness can come from someone else's success?"
-Bill Walton-

"Do what you have always done and you'll get what you have always got."
-Sue Knight-

"Think of what you have rather than of what you lack. Of the things you have, select the best and then reflect how eagerly you would have sought them if you did not have them."

-Marcus Aurelius-

"Happiness is where we find it, but very rarely where we seek it."

-J. Petit Senn-

"To be content means that you realize you contain what you seek."
-Alan Cohen-

"Expecting life to treat you well because you are a good person is like expecting an angry bull not to charge because you are a vegetarian."
-Shari R. Barr-

"View your life from your funeral: Looking back at your life experiences, what have you accomplished? What would you have wanted to accomplish but didn't? What were the happy moments? What were the sad? What would you do again, and what wouldn't you do?"
-Victor Frankl-

"Boredom is the feeling that everything is a waste of time...serenity, that nothing is."
-Thomas Szasz-

"To handle yourself, use your head; to handle others, use your heart."
-Eleanor Roosevelt-

"Don't count the days, make the days count."
-Muhammad Ali-

You may not be able to change the direction of the wind but you can adjust
your sails to reach your destination
-Jimmy Dean-

"The mediocre teacher tells. The good teacher explains. The superior teacher
demonstrates. The great teacher inspires."
-William Arthur Ward-

"Keep your fears to yourself, but share your courage with others."
-Robert Louis Stevenson-

"The greatest leader is not necessarily the one who does the greatest things.
He is the one that gets people to do the greatest things."
-Ronald Reagan-

"Power isn't control at all-power is strength, and giving that strength to

others. A leader isn't someone who forces others to make him stronger; a leader is someone willing to give his strength to others that they may have the strength to stand on their own."
-Beth Revis-

"Don't tell people how to do things; tell them what to do and let them surprise you with their results."
-George S. Patton Jr.-

"Leadership is the art of getting someone else to do something you want done because he wants to do it."
-Dwight D. Eisenhower-

"Victory has a hundred fathers and defeat is an orphan."
-John F. Kennedy-

"Management is doing things right; leadership is doing the right things."
-Peter F. Drucker-

"Example is not the main thing in influencing others. It is the only thing."
-Albert Schweitzer-

"Leaders must be close enough to relate to others, but far enough ahead to motivate them."
-John C. Maxwell-

"The mark of a great man is one who knows when to set aside the important things in order to accomplish the vital ones."
-Brandon Sanderson-

"Leadership is not about titles, positions, or flowcharts. It is about one life influencing another."
- John C. Maxwell-

"You have to be burning with an idea, or a problem, or a wrong that you want to right. If you're not passionate enough from the start, you'll never stick it out."
-Steve Jobs-

"A leader ... is like a shepherd. He stays behind the flock, letting the most nimble go out ahead, whereupon the others follow, not realizing that all along they are being directed from behind."
- Nelson Mandela-

"Light tomorrow with today."
-Elizabeth Barrett Browning-

"Being responsible sometimes means pissing people off."
-Colin Powell-

"Do you know that one of the great problems of our age is that we are governed by people who care more about feelings than they do about thoughts and ideas."
-Margaret Thatcher-

"A leader is a dealer in hope."
-Napoleon Hill-

"The best executive is the one who has sense enough to pick good men to do what he wants done, and self-restraint to keep from meddling with them while they do it."
-Theodore Roosevelt-

"If you would convince a man that he does wrong, do right. But do not care to convince him. Men will believe what they see. Let them see."
-Henry David Thoreau-

"I cannot trust a man to control others who cannot control himself."
-Robert E. Lee-

"Consensus: the process of abandoning all beliefs, principles, values, and policies in search of something in which no one believes, but to which no one objects; the process of avoiding the very issues that have to be solved, merely because you cannot get agreement on the way ahead. What great cause would have been fought and won under the banner: 'I stand for consensus?'"
-Margaret Thatcher-

"A leader takes people where they want to go. A great leader takes people where they don't necessarily want to go but ought to be."
-Rosalynn Carter-

"There is a difference between being a leader and being a boss. Both are based on authority. A boss demands blind obedience; a leader earns his authority through understanding and trust."
-Klaus Balkenhol-

"You get in life what you have the courage to ask for."
-Nancy D. Solomon-

"In the end, it is important to remember that we cannot become what we need to be by remaining what we are."
-Max De Pree-

"A leader isn't someone who forces others to make him stronger; a leader is someone willing to give his strength to others so that they may have the strength to stand on their own."
-Beth Revis-

"Always remember, Son, the best boss is the one who bosses the least. Whether it's cattle, or horses, or men, the least government is the best government."
-Ralph Moody-

"If you really want the key to success, start by doing the opposite of what everyone else is doing."
-Brad Szollose-

"Give as few orders as possible," his father had told him once long ago. "Once you've given orders on a subject, you must always give orders on that subject."
-Frank Herbert-

"The art of leadership is saying no, not yes. It is very easy to say yes."
-Tony Blair-

"Wisdom equals knowledge plus courage. You have to not only know what to do and when to do it, but you have to also be brave enough to follow through."
-Jarod Kintz-

"In a battle between two ideas, the best one doesn't necessarily win. No, the idea that wins is the one with the most fearless heretic behind it."
-Seth Godin-

"If you want to build a ship, don't drum up the men to gather wood, divide the work, and give orders. Instead, teach them to yearn for the vast and endless sea."
-Antoine de Saint-Exupery-

"Remember, teamwork begins by building trust. And the only way to do that is to overcome our need for invulnerability."
-Patrick Lencioni-

"Leadership is an action, not a position."

-Donald McGannon-

"What's money? A man is a success if he gets up in the morning and goes to bed at night and in between does what he wants to do."
-Bob Dylan-

"Even if you're on the right track, you'll get run over if you just sit there."
-Will Rogers-

"Surround yourself with great people; delegate authority; get out of the way."
-Ronald Reagan-

"I cannot give you a formula for success, but I can give you the formula for failure, which is: Try to please everybody."
-Herbert Bayard Swope-

"Show me the man you honor and I will know what kind of man you are."
-Thomas John Carlisle-

"A man always has two reasons for doing anything: a good reason and the

real reason."
-J.P. Morgan-

"If you spend your life trying to be good at everything, you will never be great at anything." **-Tom Rath-**

"Average leaders raise the bar on themselves; good leaders raise the bar for others; great leaders inspire others to raise their own bar."
-Orrin Woodward-

"Don't blow off another's candle for it won't make yours shine brighter."
-Jaachynma N.E. Agu-

"Whenever you see a successful business, someone once made a courageous decision."
-Peter F. Drucker-

"When you put together deep knowledge about a subject that intensely matters to you, charisma happens. You gain courage to share your passion, and when you do that, folks follow."
-Jerry Porras-

"People buy into the leader before they buy into the vision."
- John Maxwell-

"A good leader is a person who takes a little more than his share of the blame and a little less than his share of the credit."
- John Maxwell-

"A good plan violently executed now is better than a perfect plan executed next week."
-George Patton-

"Feeling gratitude and not expressing it is like wrapping a present and not giving it."
-William Arthur Ward-

"Start where you are. Use what you have. Do what you can."
-Arthur Ashe-

"We can easily forgive a child who is afraid of the dark; the real tragedy of life is when men are afraid of the light."
-Plato-

"Silent gratitude isn't very much to anyone."
-Gertrude Stein-

"When you come to a roadblock, take a detour."
-Mary Kay Ash-

"The only people with whom you should try to get even are those who have helped you."
-John E. Southard-

"Keep your eyes open and try to catch people in your company doing something right, then praise them for it."
-Tom Hopkins-

"Everything you've ever wanted is on the other side of fear."
-George Addair-

"You wouldn't worry so much about what others think of you if you realized how seldom they do."
-Eleanor Roosevelt-

"Low self-confidence isn't a life sentence. Self-confidence can be learned, practiced, and mastered-just like any other skill. Once you master it, everything in your life will change for the better."
-Barrie Davenport-

"Shyness has a strange element of narcissism, a belief that how we look, how we perform, is truly important to other people."
-Andre Dubus-

"You must be the change you wish to see in the world."
-Gandhi-

"Do it or not. There is no try."
-Yoda-

"When I was 5 years old, my mother always told me that happiness was the key to life. When I went to school, they asked me what I wanted to be when I grew up. I wrote down 'happy'. They told me I didn't understand the assignment, and I told them they didn't understand life."
-John Lennon-

"Every moment is a fresh beginning."
-T.S. Eliot-

"Rarely have I seen a situation where doing less than the other guy is a good strategy."
-Jimmy Spithill-

"The best revenge is massive success."
-Frank Sinatra-

"Tough times never last, but tough people do."
-Dr. Robert Schuller-

"We can easily forgive a child who is afraid of the dark; the real tragedy of life is when men are afraid of the light."
-Plato-

"The journey of a thousand miles begins with one step."
-Lao Tzu-

"The question isn't who is going to let me; it's who is going to stop me."

- Ayn Rand-

"Keep your face to the sunshine and you can never see the shadow."
-Helen Keller-

"The only way to do great work is to love what you do."
-Steve Jobs-

"Certain things catch your eye, but pursue only those that capture the heart."
-Ancient Indian Proverb-

"Everything has beauty, but not everyone can see."
-Confucius-

"How wonderful it is that nobody need wait a single moment before starting to improve the world."
-Anne Frank-

"Once you choose hope, anything's possible."
-Christopher Reeve-

"Success is going from failure to failure without losing your enthusiasm."
-Winston Churchill-

"I have been impressed with the urgency of doing. Knowing is not enough;
we must apply. Being willing is not enough; we must do."
-Leonardo da Vinci-

"When I let go of what I am, I become what I might be."
-Lao Tzu-

"Life is not measured by the number of breaths we take, but by the moments
that take our breath away."
-Maya Angelou-

"Every strike brings me closer to the next home run."
-Babe Ruth-

"Dream big and dare to fail."
-Norman Vaughan-

"Happiness is not something ready made. It comes from your own actions."
-Dalai Lama-

"What you do speaks so loudly that I cannot hear what you say."
-Ralph Waldo Emerson-

"The best way out is always through."
-Robert Frost-

"Limitations live only in our minds. But if we use our imaginations, our possibilities become limitless."
-Jamie Paolinetti-

"You must not only aim right, but draw the bow with all your might."
-Henry David Thoreau-

"If you're offered a seat on a rocket ship, don't ask what seat! Just get on."
-Sheryl Sandberg-

"The power of imagination makes us infinite."
-John Muir-

"If you want to lift yourself up, lift up someone else."
-Booker T. Washington-

"First, have a definite, clear practical ideal; a goal, an objective. Second, have the necessary means to achieve your ends; wisdom, money, materials, and methods. Third, adjust all your means to that end."
-Aristotle-

"If the wind will not serve, take to the oars."
-Latin Proverb-

"Believe you can and you're halfway there."
-Theodore Roosevelt-

"Challenges are what make life interesting and overcoming them is what makes life meaningful."
-Joshua J. Marine-

"Make each day your masterpiece."
-John Wooden-

"Don't wait. The time will never be just right."
-Napoleon Hill-

"You can't fall if you don't climb. But there's no joy in living your whole life on the ground."
-Unknown-

"We must believe that we are gifted for something, and that this thing, at whatever cost, must be attained."
-Marie Curie -

"There is only one success: to be able to spend your life in your own way."
-Christopher Morley-

"The best dreams happen when you're awake."
-Cherie Gilderbloom-

"Everything you've ever wanted is on the other side of fear."
-George Addair-

"Too many of us are not living our dreams because we are living our fears."
-Les Brown-

"You take your life in your own hands, and what happens? A terrible thing, no one to blame."
-Erica Jong-

"A year from now you may wish you had started today."
-Karen Lamb-

"Believe and act as if it were impossible to fail."
-Charles Kettering-

"The Way Get Started Is To Quit Talking And Begin Doing."

-Walt Disney-

"I didn't fail the test. I just found 100 ways to do it wrong."
-Benjamin Franklin-

"It is never too late to be what you might have been."
-George Eliot-

"In order to succeed, your desire for success should be greater than your fear of failure."
-Bill Cosby-

"The Pessimist Sees Difficulty In Every Opportunity. The Optimist Sees Opportunity In Every Difficulty."
-Winston Churchill-

"There are no traffic jams along the extra mile."
-Roger Staubach-

"Do what you can, where you are, with what you have."
-Teddy Roosevelt-

"Never let your memories be greater than your dreams."
-Doug Ivester-

"A person who never made a mistake never tried anything new."
-Albert Einstein-

"It's not whether you get knocked down, it's whether you get up."
-Vince Lombardi-

"You miss 100% of the shots you don't take."
-Wayne Gretzky-

"The person who says it cannot be done should not interrupt the person who is doing it."

-Chinese Proverb-

"There are no traffic jams along the extra mile."
-Roger Staubach-

"You Learn More From Failure Than From Success. Don't Let It Stop You.
Failure Builds Character."
-Unknown-

"It is never too late to be what you might have been."
-George Eliot-

"If You Are Working On Something That You Really Care About, You Don't
Have To Be Pushed. The Vision Pulls You."
-Steve Jobs-

"Don't wish it were easier, wish you were better."
-Jim Rohn-

"People Who Are Crazy Enough To Think They Can Change The World, Are The Ones Who Do."
-Rob Siltanen-

"You become what you believe."
-Oprah Winfrey-

"A truly rich man is one whose children run into his arms when his hands are empty."
-Unknown-

"Choosing a goal and sticking to it changes everything."
-Scott Reed-

"Entrepreneurs Are Great At Dealing With Uncertainty And Also Very Good At Minimizing Risk. That's The Classic Entrepreneur."
-Mohnish Pabrai-

"It is not what you do for your children, but what you have taught them to do for themselves, that will make them successful human beings."
-Ann Landers-

"If you want your children to turn out well, spend twice as much time with them, and half as much money."
-Abigail Van Buren-

"Build your own dreams, or someone else will hire you to build theirs."
-Farrah Gray-

"The road to Easy Street goes through the sewer."
-John Madden-

"The battles that count aren't the ones for gold medals. The struggles within yourself—the invisible battles inside all of us—that's where it's at." **-Jesse Owens-**

"If there is no struggle, there is no progress."

-Frederick Douglass-

"Education costs money. But then so does ignorance."
-Sir Claus Moser-

"I have learned over the years that when one's mind is made up, this diminishes fear."
-Rosa Parks-

"It does not matter how slowly you go as long as you do not stop."
-Confucius-

"If you look at what you have in life, you'll always have more. If you look at what you don't have in life, you'll never have enough."
-Oprah Winfrey-

"Remember that not getting what you want is sometimes a wonderful stroke of luck."
-Dalai Lama-

"You can't use up creativity. The more you use, the more you have."
-Maya Angelou-

"What we fear doing most is usually what we most need to do."
-Tim Ferriss-

"Dream big and dare to fail."
-Norman Vaughan-

"Our lives begin to end the day we become silent about things that matter."
–Martin Luther King Jr.-

"Do what you can, where you are, with what you have."
-Teddy Roosevelt-

"To avoid criticism, do nothing, say nothing, be nothing."

-Elbert Hubbard-

"If you do what you've always done, you'll get what you've always gotten."
-Tony Robbins-

"Dreaming, after all, is a form of planning."
-Gloria Steinem-

It's your place in the world; it's your life. Go on and do all you can with it, and make it the life you want to live."
-Mae Jemison-

"You may be disappointed if you fail, but you are doomed if you don't try."
-Beverly Sills-

"The more I want to get something done, the less I call it work."
-Richard Bach-

"Remember no one can make you feel inferior without your consent."
-Eleanor Roosevelt-

"Your imagination is your preview of life's coming attractions."
-Albert Einstein-

Life is what we make it, always has been, always will be.
-Grandma Moses-

"The question isn't who is going to let me; it's who is going to stop me."
-Ayn Rand-

"When everything seems to be going against you, remember that the airplane takes off against the wind, not with it."
-Henry Ford-

"Do what you love and the money will follow."
-Marsha Sinetar-

"It's not the years in your life that count. It's the life in your years."
-Abraham Lincoln-

"Change your thoughts and you change your world."
-Norman Vincent Peale-

"Either write something worth reading or do something worth writing.
-Benjamin Franklin-

"The harder I work, the luckier I get."
-Gary Player-

"You've got to bumble forward into the unknown."
-Frank Gehry-

"Nothing is impossible, the word itself says, "I'm possible!" "
-Audrey Hepburn-

"The only way to do great work is to love what you do."
-Steve Jobs-

"Even if you fall on your face, you're still moving forward."
-Victor Kiam-

"If you can dream it, you can achieve it."
-Zig Ziglar-

"The difference between ordinary and extraordinary is that little extra."
-Jimmy Johnson-

"Imagine Your Life Is Perfect In Every Respect; What Would It Look Like?"
-Brian Tracy-

"The purpose of our lives is to be happy."
-Dalai Lama-